Success With
Reading Tests

■ SCHOLASTIC

Editor: Ourania Papacharalambous
Cover design by Tannaz Fassihi; cover illustration by Kevin Zimmer
Interior design by Michelle Kim

ISBN 978-1-338-79864-7
Scholastic Inc., 557 Broadway, New York, NY 10012
Copyright © 2022 Scholastic Inc.
All rights reserved. Printed in the U.S.A.
First printing, January 2022

1 2 3 4 5 6 7 8 9 10   40   29 28 27 26 25 24 23 22

INTRODUCTION

The Scholastic Success With Reading Tests series is designed to help you help students succeed on standardized tests. In this workbook for third graders, the 10 four-page tests are culled from the reading skills practice tests provided three times a year to *Scholastic News Edition 3* subscribers, with some new and revised material. By familiarizing students with the skills, language, and formats they will encounter on state and national tests, these practice tests will boost confidence and help raise scores.

The Reading Comprehension portion of the tests measures a student's ability to read and understand different types of prose. The tests contain passages of various lengths and about various subjects. Some of the questions require students to form an understanding based on information that is explicitly stated in the passage; others require forming an understanding based on information that is only implicit in the passage.

The questions supporting each test are specifically designed to review the following skills:

- **Find the Main Idea**
- **Identify Sequence**
- **Read for Detail**
- **Identify Cause and Effect**
- **Understand Vocabulary**
- **Recognize Author's Purpose**
- **Make Inferences**
- **Identify Fact and Opinion**

The Vocabulary portion of the tests measures a student's vocabulary and varies with each test. Some tests task students with identifying synonyms and antonyms and recognizing multiple meanings; others require students to use context to choose a word that best completes a paragraph.

Note that the tests in the second half of the book are slightly more difficult. These are designed to be given later in the school year.

In addition to helping students prepare for "real" tests, the practice tests in this workbook may be used as a diagnostic tool, to help you detect individual students' strengths and weaknesses, or as an instructional tool, for oral reading and discussion.

Keep in mind that our practice tests are just that—practice. These tests are not standardized. They should not be used to determine grade level, to compare one student's performance with that of others, or to evaluate teachers' abilities.

HOW TO USE AND ADMINISTER THE TESTS

Before administering each test, you may wish to review with students some basic information as well as helpful test-taking strategies, such as reading the questions before reading the passages.

- Establish a relaxed atmosphere. Explain to students that they will not be graded and that they are taking the test to practice for "real" tests down the road.

- Encourage students to do their best, but not to worry if they don't know all the answers.

- Provide each student with a sharpened pencil with a good eraser.

- Review the directions, then read the samples in each section and discuss the answers. Be sure to pay close attention to the directions in the vocabulary section on the last page of each test.

- To mimic the atmosphere of a real test, you may wish to set time limits. Students should be able to complete the reading comprehension section (the first three pages of each test) in 20 to 25 minutes. Allow an additional 10 minutes for the vocabulary portion on the last page of each test. Encourage students to work quickly and carefully and to keep track of the remaining time—just as they would in a real testing session.

- During the test, walk around the room and, as needed, guide students to:
  - make sure that they mark one answer circle for each question.
  - be sure to read the passages before marking answers.
  - use an eraser to make any changes to answers.
  - not copy the work of other students.

- If students are taking too much time with a particular question, tell them to eliminate the answer choices that are wrong first, then to choose the answer they think is the best choice from the remaining answers. (While "guessing" is not to be encouraged, encouraging students to mark an answer, even if they are not sure, will help them make use of whatever partial knowledge they may have.)

- Watch for students who stop working before they have done all the questions and encourage them to keep working.

- Encourage students to check their work after they have finished.

At the back of this book, you will find Tested Skills charts and an Answer Key for the 10 Practice Tests. The Tested Skills charts list the core standards and skills and the test questions that measure each. The charts may be helpful to you in determining what kinds of questions students answered incorrectly, what skills they may be having trouble with, and who may need further instruction in particular skills.

Reading Skills Practice Test 1
Reading Comprehension

Read each passage. Then, fill in the circle that best completes each sentence or answers each question.

SAMPLE

Imagine drinking 500 cups of water at once. Believe it or not, that's what camels do! In the desert, water is hard to find. When a camel finds water, it drinks as much as it can. Because a camel has a big stomach, it can **gulp** down 30 gallons. That's more than 500 cups. Then it can go for several months without another drink.

1 What is the best title for this passage?
Ⓐ "Why Water Is Good for You"
Ⓑ "Life in the Desert"
Ⓒ "Thirsty Camels"
Ⓓ "Water Pollution"

2 In the passage, the word **gulp** means
Ⓐ throw.
Ⓑ drink.
Ⓒ watch.
Ⓓ walk.

A. Have you ever heard of the Man in the Moon? Many people say they can see a man's face on the surface of the moon. It's not really a face, of course. Instead, the "face" is a pattern made by **craters** and mountains on the moon's surface. When the moon is full and the sky is clear, we see some of those holes and hills.

1 What is the best title for this passage?
Ⓐ "The Moon and Stars"
Ⓑ "A Full Moon"
Ⓒ "People Land on the Moon"
Ⓓ "The Man in the Moon"

2 In this passage, the word **craters** means
Ⓐ holes.   Ⓒ mountains.
Ⓑ moons.   Ⓓ nights.

3 You can see the Man in the Moon best when the moon is
Ⓐ hidden.
Ⓑ new.
Ⓒ full.
Ⓓ flat.

4 You would probably find this passage in a
Ⓐ science book.
Ⓑ dictionary.
Ⓒ poetry book.
Ⓓ travel guide.

B. A fire can be serious. But these few simple tips can help keep you safe:

1. Put a smoke detector on every level of your home. Check the batteries once a month.

2. Make an escape plan with your family. Plan two ways to get out of each room in case of fire. Pick a spot to meet outside. Then practice!

3. If your city does not have 911, know the phone number for the fire department.

4. If there is a fire, feel a door before opening it. If it is warm, do not open it. Use another way out.

5. Crawl low, under smoke.

6. If your clothes catch fire, stop and drop to the ground. Roll around to put out the flames.

1 This passage is mainly about
- Ⓐ how most fires start.
- Ⓑ how to stay safe from fire.
- Ⓒ how to fix a smoke detector.
- Ⓓ what firefighters do.

2 If your clothes catch fire, what should you do first?
- Ⓐ stop   Ⓒ roll
- Ⓑ cry   Ⓓ run

3 You can guess from the passage that a warm door means
- Ⓐ the fire is over.
- Ⓑ the fire is close by.
- Ⓒ firefighters are on the way.
- Ⓓ the fire is small.

C. The president of the United States has one of the toughest jobs in the world. He also has one of the nicest homes.

The president lives in the White House, in Washington, D.C. This **mansion** has 132 rooms, 35 bathrooms, and 3 elevators. It also has a pool, a bowling alley, and a movie theater. It even has its own doctor's office! The president can do a lot without leaving home.

The president's home is so beautiful, it used to be called the President's Palace. President Theodore Roosevelt named it the White House in 1901.

Do you wish you owned a home like the White House? You already do! According to the U.S. Constitution, the president does not own the White House. The American people do!

1 What is the best title for this passage?
- Ⓐ "Beautiful Homes"
- Ⓑ "A New President"
- Ⓒ "The President's Home"
- Ⓓ "Write to the President"

2 In this passage, the word **mansion** means a big
- Ⓐ job.   Ⓒ car.
- Ⓑ pool.   Ⓓ home.

3 Which of these is an *opinion* about the White House?
- Ⓐ It's in Washington, D.C.
- Ⓑ It has 132 rooms.
- Ⓒ It's the nicest house in the world.
- Ⓓ It has a barbershop.

D. One African folktale tells why some spiders have bald heads. In the tale, Dog, Elephant, and other animals were having a festival to honor their parents. Anansi the spider bragged to the other animals. He said he had the best way to honor his parents. He would go a whole week without eating! The other animals groaned. They knew Anansi was a show-off.

That week, the other animals ate and ate. But Anansi got hungrier and hungrier. One day, he spotted a pot full of beans. "I will take a tiny taste," thought Anansi. "No one will know."

So Anansi took off his hat and filled it with beans. He had just begun to eat when he heard a noise. The other animals were coming! Quickly, Anansi put the hat on his head. But he forgot the hat was full of beans. The hot beans burned all the hair off Anansi's head. The other animals laughed. "Maybe this will teach Anansi to stop bragging," they said.

1 Which happened first?
Ⓐ Anansi ate the beans.
Ⓑ The beans burned Anansi's head.
Ⓒ Anansi saw the pot.
Ⓓ Anansi filled his hat.

2 The author created this passage to tell
Ⓐ that it is good to show off.
Ⓑ how to cook beans.
Ⓒ that it is wrong to brag.
Ⓓ that beans are tasty.

E. Much of our planet is covered by water. This water is always on the move. It makes a journey called the *water cycle*.

The water cycle starts when the sun's heat warms Earth's oceans and rivers. The heat makes tiny drops of water **rise** into the air. These tiny drops are called *water vapor*.

Next, the tiny drops of water gather together. They form clouds. When the clouds get too heavy, water spills out of them. The water falls back down to Earth as rain or snow. Then, the water begins its journey again.

1 In this passage, the word **rise** means
Ⓐ move up.　　Ⓒ fall.
Ⓑ move over.　　Ⓓ break.

2 What is the best title for this passage?
Ⓐ "Let It Snow!"
Ⓑ "Earth's Oceans"
Ⓒ "The Water Cycle"
Ⓓ "Types of Clouds"

3 You can guess from the passage that
Ⓐ Earth has very little water.
Ⓑ snow is made of water.
Ⓒ clouds are made of salt.
Ⓓ water never moves.

4 Which of these is a *fact*?
Ⓐ Everyone hates rain.
Ⓑ Snow is better than rain.
Ⓒ Science is boring.
Ⓓ Drops of water form clouds.

Vocabulary

Synonyms

Read the underlined word in each phrase.
Mark the word below it that has the same
(or close to the same) meaning.

Sample:
roam around
- (A) play
- (B) wander
- (C) read
- (D) see

1 speak loudly
- (A) laugh
- (B) look
- (C) talk
- (D) bend

2 allow her in
- (A) turn
- (B) let
- (C) stand
- (D) call

3 a terrible day
- (A) slow
- (B) awful
- (C) early
- (D) old

4 the correct answer
- (A) right
- (B) first
- (C) blue
- (D) wrong

5 create artwork
- (A) none
- (B) buy
- (C) drop
- (D) make

6 the fearful boy
- (A) gentle
- (B) scared
- (C) silly
- (D) kind

7 finish the chore
- (A) play
- (B) pet
- (C) job
- (D) day

Antonyms

Read the underlined word in each phrase.
Mark the word below it that means the
opposite or nearly the opposite.

Sample:
a strong person
- (A) smart
- (B) new
- (C) healthy
- (D) weak

1 a narrow hall
- (A) wide
- (B) shiny
- (C) cool
- (D) dry

2 a noisy crowd
- (A) neat
- (B) lost
- (C) quiet
- (D) big

3 load the truck
- (A) lonely
- (B) unload
- (C) pack
- (D) reload

4 many friends
- (A) real
- (B) my
- (C) few
- (D) all

5 a fancy coat
- (A) plain
- (B) short
- (C) soft
- (D) cold

6 a useful tool
- (A) powerful
- (B) wonderful
- (C) used
- (D) useless

7 a rare animal
- (A) common
- (B) ugly
- (C) wild
- (D) oily

Reading Skills Practice Test 2
Reading Comprehension

Read each passage. Then, fill in the circle that best completes each sentence or answers each question.

SAMPLE

Your nose and mouth are an open door to germs. But your tonsils stop germs before they get too far. Tonsils are like little sponges inside your throat. They soak up and **destroy** germs.

1 What is the best title for this passage?
Ⓐ "How to Be Healthy"
Ⓑ "Keep Your Nose Clean"
Ⓒ "How Your Tonsils Help You"
Ⓓ "Germs Are Bad for You"

2 In this passage, the word **destroy** means
Ⓐ hide.
Ⓑ kill.
Ⓒ see.
Ⓓ run.

A. Manatees are large water mammals. They have lived in the warm, shallow, and slow-moving waters near Florida for millions of years. But today, manatees are in danger of dying out. Many manatees get hit by motorboats. Some get tangled in fishing nets. Other manatees get sick in the winter when the water turns cold. Some scientists in Florida want to save the manatees. They have set up a special center where they take care of sick and **injured** manatees. They also rescue baby manatees whose mothers have died.

1 What is the main idea of this passage?
Ⓐ Manatees are in danger of dying out.
Ⓑ Some baby manatees need mothers.
Ⓒ Winter makes the ocean turn cold.
Ⓓ Manatees are friendly.

2 Manatees are sometimes hit by
Ⓐ scientists.
Ⓑ fishing poles.
Ⓒ ocean waves.
Ⓓ motorboats.

3 In this passage, the word **injured** means
Ⓐ wet.   Ⓒ playful.
Ⓑ hurt.   Ⓓ healthy.

B. Who Has Seen the Wind?

Who has seen the wind?
   Neither I nor you:
But when the leaves hang **trembling**
   The wind is passing through.

Who has seen the wind?
   Neither you nor I:
But when the trees bow down their heads,
   The wind is passing by.

By Christina Rossetti

1 In this poem, the word **trembling** means
  Ⓐ shaking.   Ⓒ falling.
  Ⓑ green.   Ⓓ still.

2 The leaves tremble because
  Ⓐ they are afraid.
  Ⓑ the wind is blowing on them.
  Ⓒ they are cold.
  Ⓓ they are about to dry up and fall off the tree.

3 In the poem, the trees bow down their
  Ⓐ leaves.   Ⓒ trunks.
  Ⓑ tops.   Ⓓ roots.

4 You would probably find this piece in
  Ⓐ a book about weather.
  Ⓑ a book of poetry.
  Ⓒ a science book.
  Ⓓ a book about trees.

C. Thousands of years ago, people in Egypt preserved the bodies of their dead and wrapped them in cloth called **linen**. Today, these mummies can tell scientists about how Egyptians lived in the past. In the past, scientists often had problems studying mummies. Unwrapping a mummy could easily damage it.

Now, scientists have a way to study mummies without unwrapping them. An X-ray machine called a CAT scanner takes pictures of mummies through their wraps.

The first mummy scanned was a female Egyptian mummy. The scanner took pictures of her from different angles. Then, a computer put all the pictures together to form a complete image.

1 In the passage, the word **linen** means
  Ⓐ old.   Ⓒ machine.
  Ⓑ cloth.   Ⓓ scientist.

2 The passage will likely go on to talk about
  Ⓐ what scientists learned about the mummies they scanned.
  Ⓑ how the CAT scanner was invented.
  Ⓒ machines in ancient Egypt.
  Ⓓ different kinds of cloth.

3 Which of these is a *fact*?
  Ⓐ Mummies are cool.
  Ⓑ CAT scanners are a great invention.
  Ⓒ Mummies are boring.
  Ⓓ Mummies can teach scientists about how people lived.

D. One fine summer day, some ants were hauling grain into their anthill. They were working hard to store enough grain for winter. A **merry** grasshopper came along, hopping and jumping around. He laughed at the ants. "Why are you working on such a nice day?" he asked. "You should be playing like me."

Soon, winter came. The ants had plenty to eat. One day, the grasshopper came along, looking very sad. He asked the ants to give him some grain. But the ants just laughed. "Why should we?" they said. "You played all summer while we worked hard. Now you'll go hungry while we eat."

1 In this passage, the word **merry** means
(A) sad.
(C) happy.
(B) ugly.
(D) funny.

2 You can guess from this passage that
(A) the grasshopper was lazy.
(B) the ants didn't like to have fun.
(C) real ants eat nothing but grain.
(D) grasshoppers live in meadows.

3 What happened first?
(A) Winter came.
(B) The ants stored grain.
(C) The ants laughed at the grasshopper.
(D) The grasshopper asked the ants for some grain.

E. Most people agree that trees look nice. But trees can also help cities save money. A few years ago, the U.S. Forest Service studied trees in Chicago, Illinois. They learned that just one tree can save a city $402 over the tree's lifetime.

One way trees save money is by helping us save energy. Trees shade buildings from the summer sun. They also block the winter wind. That cuts down on the energy needed to heat and cool homes and offices. This means lower bills.

Here is another way trees can help a city save money. When it rains, a city's sewers fill up with water. Cities spend lots of money to clean that water. But trees' leaves and roots soak up rainwater before it gets to the dirty sewers. With the help of trees, there is less water to clean.

1 What is the main idea of this passage?
(A) Trees are pretty.
(B) Trees block winter wind.
(C) Air pollution costs money.
(D) Trees help save money.

2 The passage will likely go on to talk about
(A) how to plant flowers.
(B) how to get cities to plant more trees.
(C) the best way to chop down a tree.
(D) forest fires.

3 Which is an *opinion* about trees?
(A) Trees block the winter wind.
(B) The tallest trees are found in cities.
(C) Trees shade buildings from sun.
(D) Trees help beautify cities.

Vocabulary

Synonyms

Read the underlined word in each phrase. Mark the word below it that has the same (or close to the same) meaning.

Sample:
<u>sip</u> lemonade
- (A) pour
- (B) drink
- (C) make
- (D) sweet

1 <u>speed</u> away
- (A) race
- (B) walk
- (C) far
- (D) slow

2 <u>gentle</u> touch
- (A) sharp
- (B) cold
- (C) soft
- (D) finger

3 <u>grumpy</u> neighbor
- (A) friendly
- (B) tall
- (C) grouchy
- (D) woman

4 <u>steam</u> carrots
- (A) chop
- (B) rabbit
- (C) eat
- (D) cook

5 loud <u>groan</u>
- (A) sound
- (B) laugh
- (C) moan
- (D) odor

6 <u>enormous</u> building
- (A) big
- (B) tired
- (C) urban
- (D) dark

7 <u>moist</u> washcloth
- (A) purple
- (B) shower
- (C) damp
- (D) dirty

Antonyms

Read the underlined word in each phrase. Mark the word below it that means the opposite or nearly the opposite.

Sample:
<u>huge</u> truck
- (A) large
- (B) red
- (C) fast
- (D) tiny

1 <u>begin</u> reading
- (A) finish
- (B) read
- (C) hard
- (D) start

2 <u>pleasant</u> weather
- (A) nice
- (B) sunny
- (C) outdoors
- (D) stormy

3 feel <u>grief</u>
- (A) sadness
- (B) comfortable
- (C) happiness
- (D) winter

4 <u>shallow</u> water
- (A) fresh
- (B) deep
- (C) pool
- (D) cold

5 <u>hind</u> leg
- (A) back
- (B) furry
- (C) front
- (D) arm

6 <u>visible</u> stain
- (A) messy
- (B) invisible
- (C) cold
- (D) new

7 <u>sink</u> in the water
- (A) trip
- (B) run
- (C) bathe
- (D) float

Reading Skills Practice Test 3
Reading Comprehension

Read each passage. Then, fill in the circle that best completes each sentence or answers each question.

SAMPLE

Weather experts use information from space to predict the weather on Earth. How? Satellites in space take pictures of Earth's atmosphere. The pictures show experts where storms are **brewing**.

1 The passage is mainly about
Ⓐ serious hurricanes.
Ⓑ weather satellites.
Ⓒ our solar system.
Ⓓ rockets.

2 In the passage, the word **brewing** means
Ⓐ finishing.   Ⓒ forming.
Ⓑ learning.   Ⓓ dripping.

A. Imagine a world where countries work together to solve problems. A group called the United Nations works to make that dream come true. The United Nations, or UN, is made up of 193 countries. It was formed in 1945, after World War II. The countries that started the UN wanted to **prevent** another big war from happening.

Today, the UN still tries to stop wars, but it has other jobs, too. UN workers bring food to people in poor countries. They try to wipe out deadly diseases. They even look for ways to help the environment.

1 In the passage the word **prevent** means
Ⓐ help.   Ⓒ stop.
Ⓑ hungry.   Ⓓ begin.

2 The best title for this passage is
Ⓐ "All About World War II."
Ⓑ "All About the UN."
Ⓒ "How to Help Earth."
Ⓓ "How to Stop Wars."

3 Which of these happened last?
Ⓐ The UN was formed.
Ⓑ World War II ended.
Ⓒ Wold War II started.
Ⓓ The UN began to help poor countries.

4 You can guess from the passage that
Ⓐ the UN started World War II.
Ⓑ peace is important to the UN.
Ⓒ the United States does not belong to the UN.
Ⓓ every country in the world belongs to the UN.

B. Do your feet stink after you exercise? The bad smell comes from microbes, or living things that grow on your skin. Microbes are very small. You can only see them with a microscope. But they have big names. One is called **corynebacteria**.

Microbes are all over your body. But they grow best on skin that is sweaty and warm. That's why feet smell after you exercise.

1 This passage is mainly about
Ⓐ why you exercise.
Ⓑ why feet smell.
Ⓒ how to use a microscope.
Ⓓ how microbes are named.

2 **Corynebacteria** is a kind of
Ⓐ sneaker.   Ⓒ kid.
Ⓑ exercise.   Ⓓ microbe.

3 Your feet smell because
Ⓐ microbes grow on them.
Ⓑ you use old soap.
Ⓒ they are too big.
Ⓓ they are funny looking.

4 You can guess from the passage that
Ⓐ exercise is bad for your health.
Ⓑ there are microbes on your face and hands.
Ⓒ you should wash your feet three times a day.
Ⓓ microbes are green and slimy.

C. Once, only kids at private schools wore uniforms. Now, many public schools ask students to wear uniforms. It has caused a big debate.

Many students like wearing uniforms. They say it is easy to get dressed in the morning. And families have to buy only one or two uniforms, instead of a closet full of clothes.

Not everyone likes school uniforms, though. Some people say it's not fair to make kids wear the same thing.

1 The main idea of the passage is that school uniforms
Ⓐ are more expensive than regular clothes.
Ⓑ are less expensive than regular clothes.
Ⓒ have caused a big debate.
Ⓓ look nice.

2 Today, uniforms are worn
Ⓐ only at private schools.
Ⓑ only at public schools.
Ⓒ at many private and public schools.
Ⓓ only in other countries.

3 The author probably wrote this passage to
Ⓐ persuade students to wear uniforms.
Ⓑ give both sides of the uniform debate.
Ⓒ stop children from wearing uniforms.
Ⓓ help schools create new uniforms.

D. The story of Paul Bunyan is a famous American legend. It was first told in the early 1900s.

According to the legend, Paul Bunyan was a giant. Paul's parents knew he was going to be big right from the start. When he was only one week old, he wore his father's clothes! He would eat 40 bowls of porridge at one meal.

For his first birthday, Paul got a **huge** blue ox named Babe. Babe and Paul played in the woods. They were so heavy that their footprints formed lakes.

When Paul grew up, he became a lumberjack. He could cut down a whole forest by himself. Once, he formed the Grand Canyon by dragging his tools behind him!

1 In the passage, the word **huge** means
Ⓐ large. Ⓒ blue.
Ⓑ hungry. Ⓓ smart.

2 Which of these happened first?
Ⓐ Paul became a lumberjack.
Ⓑ Paul wore his father's clothes.
Ⓒ Paul formed the Grand Canyon.
Ⓓ Paul got a blue ox.

3 You can guess that
Ⓐ Paul Bunyan lived in Florida.
Ⓑ Paul Bunyan lived in 1850.
Ⓒ the legend is not really true.
Ⓓ footprints can form lakes.

E. Riding a bike can be fun, but it's important to stay safe. Here are some tips for safe cycling:
- Always wear a bicycle helmet that fits your head. If you fall, it can protect your head from serious injuries.
- Never ride a bike after dark.
- If you are under age 10, do not ride in the street without an adult. When you do ride in the street, use hand signals to show where you are going. Obey stop signs and other traffic rules.
- Wear bright clothing when you ride so that drivers, walkers, and other bicyclists can **spot** you.
- Do not ride a bike that is too large for you, or one that is not in good working order.

1 The passage is mainly about
Ⓐ traffic rules. Ⓒ bike safety.
Ⓑ tricycles. Ⓓ sports.

2 Bike riders should wear clothes that are
Ⓐ bright. Ⓒ loose.
Ⓑ tight. Ⓓ dark.

3 In the passage, the word **spot** means
Ⓐ see. Ⓒ dog.
Ⓑ mark. Ⓓ help.

4 You would probably find this passage in a book about
Ⓐ driving.
Ⓑ safety.
Ⓒ clothing.
Ⓓ folk tales.

Vocabulary

Synonyms

Read the underlined word in each phrase. Mark the word below it that has the same (or close to the same) meaning.

Sample:

speak loudly
- (A) look
- (B) fly
- (C) talk
- (D) cry

1 shut the door
- (A) ring
- (B) knock
- (C) open
- (D) close

2 giant creature
- (A) tiny
- (B) scary
- (C) large
- (D) animal

3 reply soon
- (A) return
- (B) swim
- (C) answer
- (D) mind

4 shall go
- (A) will
- (B) never
- (C) please
- (D) back

5 intelligent student
- (A) new
- (B) smart
- (C) alone
- (D) old

6 wander around
- (A) fold
- (B) roam
- (C) soak
- (D) let

7 shred paper
- (A) raise
- (B) news
- (C) rip
- (D) draw

Antonyms

Read the underlined word in each phrase. Mark the word below it that means the opposite or nearly the opposite.

Sample:

lay asleep
- (A) fast
- (B) worried
- (C) still
- (D) awake

1 straight line
- (A) nice
- (B) crooked
- (C) dark
- (D) lost

2 wrong answer
- (A) check
- (B) mark
- (C) right
- (D) last

3 sweet taste
- (A) sugary
- (B) sour
- (C) chocolate
- (D) cold

4 terrible day
- (A) great
- (B) bad
- (C) long
- (D) early

5 frown on her face
- (A) spill
- (B) mad
- (C) smile
- (D) nose

6 tight coat
- (A) loose
- (B) blue
- (C) warm
- (D) small

7 worst thing
- (A) stop
- (B) best
- (C) kind
- (D) past

Reading Skills Practice Test 4
Reading Comprehension

Read each passage. Then, fill in the circle that best completes each sentence or answers each question.

SAMPLE

You can guess the meaning of some words by the way the words sound. For example, the word "squeak" sounds like a squeak. The word "cackle" sounds like a person cackling. The term for these "sound words" is onomatopoeia. It is fun to use sound words when you write.

1 The best title for this passage is
Ⓐ "Be a Good Writer."
Ⓑ "Using a Dictionary."
Ⓒ "Sound Words."
Ⓓ "Rhyming Words."

2 You can guess from the passage that _____ is a sound word.
Ⓐ "hiss"   Ⓒ "spoon"
Ⓑ "plant"   Ⓓ "sister"

A. Everyone knows about the telephone, the car, and the electric light. People use these inventions every day. But there are other inventions that few people have heard of. For example, one inventor **created** a twirling fork to make it easier to eat spaghetti. Another invented diapers for pet birds. And someone else invented a sleeping bag with leg holes. Why? The holes let a camper run away when a bear comes along!

1 A good title for this passage is
Ⓐ "More Spaghetti!"
Ⓑ "Unusual Inventions."
Ⓒ "Famous Inventions."
Ⓓ "Pet Supplies."

2 In the passage, the word **created** means
Ⓐ ate.   Ⓒ twirled.
Ⓑ ran away.   Ⓓ made.

3 You can guess from the passage that
Ⓐ more people own cars than twirling forks.
Ⓑ most people have twirling forks.
Ⓒ all campers hate bears.
Ⓓ the person who invented bird diapers is famous.

4 Which of these is an *opinion*?
Ⓐ People use telephones and cars.
Ⓑ Someone invented a twirling fork.
Ⓒ It's silly to make diapers for pets.
Ⓓ Some sleeping bags have leg holes.

Name _____ Date _____

B. Imagine giving stitches to sheep or taking a tiger's temperature. That's what a veterinarian, or animal doctor, does.

There are more than 70,000 veterinarians in the United States. Some take care of pets like dogs, cats, and hamsters. Others care for farm animals like horses and cows. Still other vets work at zoos. They get to help care for elephants, zebras, gorillas, and other less common creatures.

Being a vet is not easy. Veterinarians go to college for at least eight years to learn about animals. They often work more than 50 hours a week. But many veterinarians say that their **career** is exciting and fun.

1 Approximately how many veterinarians are in the U.S.?
Ⓐ 12,000 Ⓒ 70,000
Ⓑ 40,000 Ⓓ 6,000

2 In the passage, the word **career** means
Ⓐ job. Ⓒ patient.
Ⓑ cat. Ⓓ stitches.

3 Being a vet is hard because a vet often
Ⓐ does not go to college.
Ⓑ works many hours a week.
Ⓒ does not earn any money.
Ⓓ hates dogs and cats.

C. In February of 1962, John Glenn made space history. This American astronaut climbed aboard a tiny space capsule called *Friendship 7*. He traveled 160 miles above Earth. Glenn orbited the planet three times, then safely returned to Earth. He was the first American astronaut to circle Earth.

In October of 1998, John Glenn again blasted into space. He served as a specialist on board the space shuttle *Discovery*. Glenn studied the effects of space flight on older people.

John Glenn received the Presidential Medal of Freedom on May 29, 2012.

1 This passage is mostly about
Ⓐ space missions of the 1960s.
Ⓑ astronauts of today.
Ⓒ John Glenn's space flights.
Ⓓ different kinds of spacecraft.

2 When did Glenn travel on the *Friendship 7*?
Ⓐ October of 1962
Ⓑ October of 1998
Ⓒ February of 1962
Ⓓ February of 1998

3 Which happened last?
Ⓐ Glenn traveled on the *Discovery*.
Ⓑ Glenn climbed on board the *Friendship 7*.
Ⓒ Glenn became the first American to orbit Earth.
Ⓓ Glenn recieved the Presidential Medal of Freedom.

D. Crayons have been around for more than a hundred years. But they have changed a lot. The first crayons were all black. Workers in shipyards used them to label crates. Then, in the early 1900s, the Crayola company decided to make colorful crayons for kids. The first box had eight colors: black, brown, red, blue, purple, orange, yellow, and green. The box cost just five cents.

Today, there are hundreds of crayon colors, from "tickle me pink" to "tropical rain forest." Scientists keep blending different colors to come up with new shades. Then the scientists show the new color to kids to see if they will use it. Crayon companies have also asked children to help name new crayon colors.

1 This passage is mostly about
Ⓐ rain forests.　　Ⓒ rainbows.
Ⓑ scientists.　　Ⓓ crayons.

2 You can guess from the passage that
Ⓐ a box of crayons costs more than five cents today.
Ⓑ crayon companies no longer make plain red crayons.
Ⓒ no one uses crayons anymore.
Ⓓ "tropical rain forest" is a shade of blue.

3 The passage will likely go on to talk about
Ⓐ shipyard workers.
Ⓑ kids' favorite crayon colors.
Ⓒ the history of paper.
Ⓓ the first crayons.

E. Respect Them, Protect Them

Splish, splash! Splish, splash!
Fish frolic in the seas.
Swish, swoosh! Swish, swoosh!
Birds fly in the breeze.
Scritch, scratch! Scritch, scratch!
Crabs dig in the sand.
Romp, stomp! Romp, stomp!
Animals roam the land.
Seas, breeze, sand, land.
There are creatures everywhere.
Respect them, **protect** them
On this planet that we share.

By Karen Kellaher

1 In the poem, the word **protect** means
Ⓐ keep safe.　　Ⓒ know.
Ⓑ see.　　Ⓓ dig.

2 You'd probably find this poem in a
Ⓐ book of autumn poems.
Ⓑ book of animal poems.
Ⓒ book of New Year's poems.
Ⓓ book of Halloween poems

3 The poet probably wrote the poem
Ⓐ to convince kids to study hard in school.
Ⓑ to teach people about crabs.
Ⓒ to celebrate winter.
Ⓓ to convince people to help animals.

Vocabulary
Which Word Is Missing?

In each of the following paragraphs, a word is missing. First, read the paragraph. Then, find the missing word in the list of words beneath the paragraph. Fill in the circle next to the word that is missing.

Sample:

I have a lot of homework, so I should get started on it _____.

Ⓐ someday   Ⓒ soon

Ⓑ maybe   Ⓓ later

1 Icy Antarctica is not an easy place to live. In summer, this continent has an average temperature of zero degrees. In winter, the temperature can drop to 100 degrees below zero! Brrrr! Few creatures can live in such _____ conditions.

Ⓐ cold   Ⓒ strange

Ⓑ warm   Ⓓ ugly

2 Penguins do not seem to mind the cold. These birds live along the coast of Antarctica. They spend some time on land, but most of their time is spent in the chilly _____ around Antarctica.

Ⓐ birds   Ⓒ lands

Ⓑ feathers   Ⓓ waters

3 How do penguins stay warm? They have a thick layer of fat called blubber. And they have oily black and white _____ to keep the icy water away from their skin.

Ⓐ windows   Ⓒ feathers

Ⓑ head   Ⓓ eyes

4 Penguins cannot _____ like most birds. Instead, they waddle around on two feet. Sometimes they slide on the ice on their stomachs.

Ⓐ read   Ⓒ eat

Ⓑ fly   Ⓓ see

5 In the ocean, penguins can dive _____ under the water. They swim by opening and closing their wings and paddling their feet.

Ⓐ never   Ⓒ deep

Ⓑ late   Ⓓ walk

6 Penguins live in groups. Mothers lay their eggs in a spot called a rookery. There can be thousands of penguins in one rookery. Even in the ocean, penguins stick _____.

Ⓐ home   Ⓒ alone

Ⓑ together   Ⓓ cousin

7 Penguins don't eat a lot. They usually munch on fish and tiny creatures called krill. When they are very _____, they might eat a squid.

Ⓐ hungry   Ⓒ cold

Ⓑ tired   Ⓓ gone

Reading Skills Practice Test 5
Reading Comprehension

Read each passage. Then, fill in the circle that best completes each sentence or answers each question.

SAMPLE

Dolphins are sea animals. However, they are not fish and cannot breathe in water. Like whales, dolphins are mammals. They must come up to the **surface** to breathe air. Dolphins travel through the sea in large groups.

1 What is the best title for this passage?
Ⓐ "Breathing"
Ⓑ "Fish"
Ⓒ "Dolphins"
Ⓓ "Animals"

2 In this passage, the word **surface** means
Ⓐ the top of the water.
Ⓑ the bottom of the sea.
Ⓒ an ocean rock.
Ⓓ a sea plant.

A. To a bat, the world must seem topsy-turvy. That's because this creature spends a good part of its day hanging upside down! A bat has five sharp claws on each of its short **hind** legs. It uses the claws to hang upside down from tree branches, caves, and city bridges. A bat hangs for many hours each day—even while it is sleeping, eating, and washing itself. In fact, the only time this flying mammal is right side up is when it is fetching insects, fruit, or other meals.

1 In this passage, the word **hind** means
Ⓐ flying.   Ⓒ dry.
Ⓑ imaginary.   Ⓓ back.

2 The passage is mainly about
Ⓐ how bats find food.
Ⓑ how bats hang upside down.
Ⓒ bats and other mammals.
Ⓓ all kinds of caves.

3 A bat is right side up when it
Ⓐ finds food.   Ⓒ washes itself.
Ⓑ sleeps.   Ⓓ eats.

4 This passage will likely go on to talk about
Ⓐ baby bats.
Ⓑ a bat's sense of smell.
Ⓒ a bat's eyesight.
Ⓓ the types of foods bats eat.

B. He was born in Italy more than 500 years ago. He is known as one of the world's greatest artists. But Leonardo da Vinci might also be one of the smartest people who ever lived.

People who have studied Leonardo's notebooks can't believe what they've found. Leonardo's drawings show that he was a scientist, an astronomer, and an engineer. He had ideas about how waves form, why the moon shines, and how flying machines might work. Though no one knows why, Leonardo wrote all his ideas down backward! You need a mirror to read his writing.

1 The main idea of the passage is that Leonardo da Vinci
Ⓐ liked watching the moon.
Ⓑ may be one of the smartest people who ever lived.
Ⓒ lived a very long time ago.
Ⓓ was an astronomer.

2 Leonardo da Vinci was born in
Ⓐ Italy.   Ⓒ England.
Ⓑ the U.S.   Ⓓ France.

3 You need a mirror to read Leonardo da Vinci's writing because
Ⓐ he had messy handwriting.
Ⓑ he wrote by moonlight.
Ⓒ he wrote in pictures instead of words.
Ⓓ he wrote backward.

C. Venus is sometimes called Earth's sister, or twin. That's because it is the planet **nearest** to Earth. It's also about the same size as Earth.

But Venus is different from Earth in many ways. Venus is much hotter than Earth. It is about 850 degrees on Venus's surface! The air, or atmosphere, around Venus is thick and heavy. It's so thick you can't even see through it. This air traps the sun's heat.

1 What is the best title for this passage?
Ⓐ "Nine Planets"
Ⓑ "Hot Air"
Ⓒ "Sisters"
Ⓓ "Earth's Hot Twin"

2 One reason Venus is called Earth's twin is because
Ⓐ they are both planets.
Ⓑ they are both very hot.
Ⓒ they are about the same size.
Ⓓ they have the same air.

3 In this passage, the word **nearest** means
Ⓐ hottest.
Ⓑ closest.
Ⓒ driest.
Ⓓ roundest.

4 The passage will likely go on to talk about
Ⓐ Jupiter's similarity to Earth.
Ⓑ Venus's similarity to other planets.
Ⓒ the history of Earth.
Ⓓ more facts that scientists have learned about Venus.

D. Each year in Japan, children celebrate *Undokai*, or Sports Day. On this special day, schools compete against each other in relay races and other track events. One favorite race is the *daruma*. In this event, runners race in pairs. One runner in the pair wears something over his or her head, making it impossible to see. This runner is **guided** by his or her partner, who carries a small ball on a scoop. If the ball drops, the pair of runners must start the race over!

1 What is the best title for this passage?
Ⓐ "Races Through History"
Ⓑ "Sports Day in Japan"
Ⓒ "Japan Today"
Ⓓ "Teams"

2 Who competes on Sports Day?
Ⓐ children
Ⓑ parents
Ⓒ professional athletes
Ⓓ teachers

3 In this passage, the word **guided** means
Ⓐ won.   Ⓒ followed.
Ⓑ led.   Ⓓ copied.

4 You can guess from the passage that
Ⓐ children in Japan study a lot.
Ⓑ daruma is the first event.
Ⓒ Undokai is a popular day.
Ⓓ students must run barefoot.

E. A bike helmet is made of hard foam. The foam absorbs the force of a fall so that the hard ground does not hurt your head. But your helmet won't protect your head if it doesn't fit right. Here are some tips for **selecting** the best helmet.
• Try on helmets at a bike store. Pick one that isn't too tight. But make sure it isn't so big that it rocks back and forth.
• Most helmets come with soft pads. Stick the pads on the inside of the helmet to make it fit just right.
• Keep the front of your helmet just above your eyebrows when you ride.
• Make sure the chin strap fits snugly under your chin. The strap holds the helmet on if you are in an accident.

1 In this passage, the word **selecting** means
Ⓐ wearing.   Ⓒ choosing.
Ⓑ riding.   Ⓓ cleaning.

2 Bike helmets are needed because
Ⓐ all bike riders go too fast.
Ⓑ kids are careless.
Ⓒ they protect your head.
Ⓓ they keep your head warm.

3 Which of these is an *opinion* about helmets?
Ⓐ They are made of hard foam.
Ⓑ Most come with soft pads.
Ⓒ They have chin straps.
Ⓓ They are attractive.

Vocabulary

Synonyms

Read the underlined word in each phrase.
Mark the word below it that has the same
(or close to the same) meaning.

Sample:

mend the sweater
- (A) rip
- (B) raise
- (C) wear
- (D) fix

1 discover treasure
- (A) bury
- (B) find
- (C) golden
- (D) pirate

2 false alarm
- (A) loud
- (B) long
- (C) mistaken
- (D) true

3 receive a gift
- (A) get
- (B) give
- (C) lose
- (D) wrap

4 old custom
- (A) trunk
- (B) clothes
- (C) money
- (D) tradition

5 long silence
- (A) quiet
- (B) storm
- (C) light
- (D) package

6 complete the test
- (A) finish
- (B) fail
- (C) lose
- (D) write

7 scent of roses
- (A) field
- (B) store
- (C) color
- (D) smell

Multiple Meanings

Read each set of sentences. Mark the word
that makes sense in both sentences.

Sample:

The doctor put the girl's broken leg
in a _____.
The _____ of that movie is
very talented.
- (A) cast
- (B) sling
- (C) actor
- (D) station

1 Can you help me _____ a shirt?
The machine is made of _____.
- (A) play
- (B) wash
- (C) iron
- (D) find

2 I would love another _____
of stew.
He is known for _____ others.
- (A) share
- (B) plate
- (C) teaching
- (D) helping

3 The man helped his mother _____
the bus.
The students made a bulletin
_____ for winter.
- (A) board
- (B) ride
- (C) catch
- (D) poster

4 There is a _____ on your shirt.
If you _____ a parking space,
let me know.
- (A) stain
- (B) spot
- (C) see
- (D) button

Reading Skills Practice Test 6
Reading Comprehension

Read each passage. Then, fill in the circle that best completes each sentence or answers each question.

SAMPLE

Mars is called the Red Planet. That's because the **soil** on Mars has a lot of rust. Rust is the same substance that forms on a bicycle left out in the rain. The rusty dirt makes Mars look red.

1 The best title for this passage is
Ⓐ "Mars: The Orange Planet."
Ⓑ "Mars: The Red Planet."
Ⓒ "Take Care of Your Bike."
Ⓓ "Plants on Mars."

2 In the passage, the word **soil** means
Ⓐ air.
Ⓑ bike.
Ⓒ dirt.
Ⓓ red.

A. Imagine a music group that has no guitars, pianos, or drums. Instead, its members make music with brooms, trash cans, and pot lids!

Believe it or not, this **odd** group really exists. It is called *Stomp*. *Stomp* started in England in 1991. Since then, it has performed all over the world. It is famous for its lively music and funny shows.

1 The best title for this passage is
Ⓐ "Playing the Piano."
Ⓑ "The History of Music."
Ⓒ "*Stomp*'s Unusual Music."
Ⓓ "English Musicians."

2 The members of *Stomp* play
Ⓐ guitars.   Ⓒ flutes.
Ⓑ trash cans.   Ⓓ pianos.

3 In the passage, the word **odd** means
Ⓐ helpful.   Ⓒ old.
Ⓑ lost.   Ⓓ unusual.

4 You would probably find this passage
Ⓐ in a magazine about music.
Ⓑ in a history book.
Ⓒ in a book about pianos.
Ⓓ in a geography book.

5 Which of these is an *opinion*?
Ⓐ *Stomp* started in England.
Ⓑ *Stomp*'s music is too loud.
Ⓒ *Stomp* does not use drums.
Ⓓ *Stomp* began in 1991.

B. In the 1800s, American women were not allowed to vote. Many people fought to change that. They were called *suffragists*.

One famous suffragist was Elizabeth Cady Stanton. In 1848, she planned a meeting called the Seneca Falls Convention. More than 100 people met to talk about women's rights. Stanton **spoke** to them. She said that "men and women are created equal."

In 1878, lawmakers finally listened to Stanton and the other suffragists. They started talking about changing the law to give women the right to vote. The law finally changed 42 years later.

1 This passage is mainly about
Ⓐ Susan B. Anthony.
Ⓑ Elizabeth Cady Stanton.
Ⓒ the history of the United States.
Ⓓ many famous women.

2 The Seneca Falls Convention was in
Ⓐ 1800. Ⓒ 1848.
Ⓑ 1828. Ⓓ 1878.

3 In the passage, the word **spoke** means
Ⓐ talked. Ⓒ went.
Ⓑ found. Ⓓ helped.

4 You can guess from this passage that
Ⓐ Stanton didn't think men should have the right to vote.
Ⓑ Stanton was very rich.
Ⓒ American women can vote today.
Ⓓ lawmakers did not like Stanton.

C. Do you love to ride on a racing roller coaster? You are not alone. Roller coasters have been thrilling riders for hundreds of years!

Roller coasters got their start in Russia 600 years ago. Back then, there were no lightning-fast loops. Instead, riders just slid down icy mountains. By 1700, people were making rides that used tracks and wheels instead of ice.

The first American coaster was built in Coney Island, New York, in 1884. It was the Switchback Railway. It looked like a train going down a mountain. Soon, other parks made similar rides, and roller coasters really took off!

1 The first American roller coaster was called the
Ⓐ Loop-A-Rama.
Ⓑ Coney Island.
Ⓒ Superdrop.
Ⓓ Switchback Railway.

2 Which of these happened *first*?
Ⓐ An American coaster was built.
Ⓑ Russian people slid down icy mountains.
Ⓒ Coasters started using wheels.
Ⓓ The Switchback Railway opened.

3 The passage will likely go on to talk about
Ⓐ today's roller coasters.
Ⓑ weather in Russia.
Ⓒ where Coney Island is located.
Ⓓ railroads of the world.

D. Most people have never heard of Patty Smith Hill. But almost everyone knows this songwriter's famous work!

Patty Smith Hill was a teacher who lived in Kentucky more than 100 years ago. In 1893, she was **searching** for songs for children to sing at school. She decided to write one of her own. She wrote words to a song and called it "Good Morning to All." Smith's sister, Mildred, wrote some music to go with the words.

Schoolchildren loved the sisters' song. In 1924, the Smiths added a new verse to the song. It was called, "Happy Birthday to You." Sound familiar? It's now one of the most famous songs in the world!

1 This passage is mostly about
Ⓐ the history of a popular song.
Ⓑ children around the world.
Ⓒ living in Kentucky.
Ⓓ how people can work together.

2 Patty Smith Hill wrote the "Happy Birthday" song with her
Ⓐ father.   Ⓒ brother.
Ⓑ mother.   Ⓓ sister.

3 In the passage, the word **searching** means
Ⓐ singing.   Ⓒ driving.
Ⓑ looking.   Ⓓ knowing.

4 The author probably wrote the passage
Ⓐ to get readers to sing.
Ⓑ to celebrate his or her birthday.
Ⓒ to make Patty Smith Hill happy.
Ⓓ to give readers some history.

E. For six states in the middle of our country, springtime brings more than birds and flowers. It also brings tornadoes.

Tornadoes, or twisters, can strike almost anywhere. But many tornadoes happen in Texas, Oklahoma, Kansas, Nebraska, Iowa, and Missouri. These states are called Tornado Alley.

A tornado is a spinning column of air that forms from a thunderstorm. Inside a tornado, air spins at nearly 300 miles per hour. The spinning air acts like a vacuum. It can uproot trees and make cars fly through the air.

The United States has hundreds of tornadoes every year. Luckily, only a few of them are strong enough to cause damage.

1 You can guess from the passage that
Ⓐ most tornadoes happen in fall.
Ⓑ "twister" is another word for tornado.
Ⓒ Iowa gets more tornadoes than Kansas does.
Ⓓ Missouri does not get tornadoes.

2 A tornado's spinning air can cause
Ⓐ thunderstorms to begin.
Ⓑ flowers to bloom.
Ⓒ springtime to start early.
Ⓓ cars to fly through the air.

3 Which is a *fact* about tornadoes?
Ⓐ They are scarier than blizzards.
Ⓑ They are interesting to study.
Ⓒ They often happen in spring.
Ⓓ They should be called "spinners."

Vocabulary

Synonyms

Read the underlined word in each phrase. Mark the word below it that has the same (or close to the same) meaning.

Sample:
a huge <u>feast</u>
- Ⓐ letter
- Ⓒ lawn
- Ⓑ wish
- Ⓓ meal

1 <u>frighten</u> him
- Ⓐ ask
- Ⓒ draw
- Ⓑ scare
- Ⓓ pull

2 a long <u>battle</u>
- Ⓐ year
- Ⓒ fight
- Ⓑ bag
- Ⓓ nail

3 a fire <u>blazed</u>
- Ⓐ cleaned
- Ⓒ fell
- Ⓑ stopped
- Ⓓ burned

4 a feeling of <u>joy</u>
- Ⓐ fear
- Ⓒ anger
- Ⓑ happiness
- Ⓓ sadness

5 don't <u>disturb</u> her
- Ⓐ bother
- Ⓒ smile
- Ⓑ let
- Ⓓ grow

6 <u>calm</u> sea
- Ⓐ peaceful
- Ⓒ far
- Ⓑ my
- Ⓓ locked

7 famous <u>author</u>
- Ⓐ meal
- Ⓒ eat
- Ⓑ driver
- Ⓓ writer

Multiple Meanings

Read each set of sentences. Mark the word that makes sense in both sentences.

Sample:
Margaret is a stylish _____.
I have a new _____ in my bedroom.
- Ⓐ painting
- Ⓒ dresser
- Ⓑ bed
- Ⓓ door

1 I was so hungry, I felt like I might _____.
We could see very _____ numbers on the old mailbox.
- Ⓐ starve
- Ⓒ low
- Ⓑ faint
- Ⓓ many

2 I _____ my spelling book at school.
Gregory writes with his _____ hand.
- Ⓐ right
- Ⓒ bought
- Ⓑ leave
- Ⓓ left

3 My neighbor asked me to _____ her dog while she's on vacation.
Katie looked like something was on her _____.
- Ⓐ shirt
- Ⓒ keep
- Ⓑ mind
- Ⓓ feed

4 The runners jog around the _____.
Our teacher told us to keep _____ of how much we read each night.
- Ⓐ school
- Ⓒ track
- Ⓑ records
- Ⓓ street

Reading Skills Practice Test 7
Reading Comprehension

Read each passage. Then, fill in the circle that best completes each sentence or answers each question.

SAMPLE

What does your last name say about you? If you lived in England in the 1100s, it told others what you did for a living. For example, people in the Parker family were park keepers, and the Baker **clan** actually baked bread and cakes! The Walls were builders, while the Smiths were blacksmiths. If your family's name is one of these, you may have a clue about how your ancestors earned a living!

1 What is the best title for this passage?
Ⓐ "Make a Family Tree"
Ⓑ "Names Tell Stories"
Ⓒ "How to Choose a Job"
Ⓓ "Builders of Long Ago"

2 In this passage, the word **clan** means
Ⓐ time.
Ⓑ clue.
Ⓒ family.
Ⓓ bread.

A. Here's some good news for pizza lovers! Pizza is not just tasty, it also provides important nutrients your body needs. Tomatoes, cheese, and wheat all contain vitamins to keep your body healthy and strong. Add some mushrooms or peppers on top, and you'll pack in even more vitamins. Cheese has protein, which your body uses to grow and **repair** cells. Pizza dough has plenty of carbohydrates—the nutrients that give you energy to play and learn. And, last but not least, the cheese and oil on pizza have fats, which your body needs to store energy over time. Of course, too much fat is bad for your heart, so it's smart to save pizza for a special treat.

1 This passage is mainly about
Ⓐ ways to serve pizza.
Ⓑ kids' favorite pizza toppings.
Ⓒ the invention of pizza.
Ⓓ the nutrients in pizza.

2 In this passage, the word **repair** means
Ⓐ fix.   Ⓒ eat.
Ⓑ lose.   Ⓓ cook.

3 Cheese and oil both contain
Ⓐ protein.   Ⓒ pizza.
Ⓑ fat.   Ⓓ carbohydrates.

4 You can guess from the passage that
Ⓐ you should never eat pizza.
Ⓑ you should not eat pizza every day.
Ⓒ pizza is very hard to make.
Ⓓ pizza has 20 different ingredients.

Name _____ Date _____

B. In dinosaur movies and TV shows, dinos hiss, hoot, screech, and roar. But in real life, paleontologists, or dinosaur experts, don't know what kinds of sounds dinosaurs made. However, they can make some guesses based on studies of dino skulls.

Paleontologists say that many dinos had pointy crests on their heads. These hollow crests would have filled with air when the dinosaur breathed. As air moved through the crest, the dinosaur probably made a deep bellowing or roaring sound.

Experts also say that dinosaurs probably had good reasons to make noise. Like other creatures, dinos probably made sounds to warn fellow dinosaurs away from danger, to find mates, and to communicate with their young.

1 This passage is mainly about
(A) how paleontologists work.
(B) dinosaur skeletons.
(C) how dinosaurs breathed.
(D) the noises dinosaurs made.

2 According to the passage, which of these is probably *not* a reason for dinosaurs to have made noise?
(A) to warn fellow dinos from danger
(B) to find mates
(C) to entertain each other
(D) to communicate with their young

3 A sound probably occurred as air moved through the dinosaur's
(A) body. (C) nostrils.
(B) crest. (D) mouth.

C. If you like talking to people and writing stories, being a news reporter may be the job for you. It is challenging, though! Reporters work hard and face tough deadlines. They follow four steps to finish a news story:

1. Do research. When reporters learn about a news event, they gather facts. They **interview** people involved in the event and take careful notes. They try to answer the questions *who, what, when, where, why,* and *how.*
2. Write the lead. The lead of a news story is the first sentence or several sentences. The lead tells the most important idea of the story and makes the reader want to keep reading.
3. Write the body of the story. The body, or main part, of the story gives details that support the lead sentence. Sometimes, the body contains quotes from the people interviewed by the reporter.
4. Write a headline. A headline is the title of a news story. It should summarize the main idea of the story and grab the reader's attention.

1 What is the best title for this passage?
(A) "This Week's Top News"
(B) "How Reporters Write Stories"
(C) "Writing Good Headlines"
(D) "The Research Process"

2 The first sentence or sentences of a news story is called the
(A) body. (C) lead.
(B) interview. (D) caption.

© Scholastic Inc.

D. The Robin

A Mother Goose Rhyme

The north wind doth blow,
And we **shall** have snow,
And what will the robin do then,
                          Poor thing?

He'll sit in a barn,
And keep himself warm,
And hide his head under his wing,
                          Poor thing!

1 Another good title for this poem might be
Ⓐ "A Robin's Nest."
Ⓑ "A Robin in Winter."
Ⓒ "The North Wind."
Ⓓ "Snow Is on the Way."

2 In this poem, the word **shall** means
Ⓐ flies.   Ⓒ will.
Ⓑ hope.   Ⓓ did.

3 The poet probably created this rhyme to
Ⓐ entertain people.
Ⓑ entertain robins.
Ⓒ explain snowfall.
Ⓓ celebrate springtime.

4 You can guess from the poem that
Ⓐ robins only live where it's cold.
Ⓑ robins enjoy cold weather.
Ⓒ the poet feels sorry for robins.
Ⓓ the poet dislikes robins.

E. Loch Ness is a lake in northern Scotland. It is also home to a famous story—the legend of the Loch Ness Monster.

The legend began around 565 C.E. That's when people near the lake first began talking about a strange sea beast. Then, in 1933, a couple said they saw a giant creature tossing and turning in the lake. Newspapers all over the world reported the strange event.

Since then, about 20 people a year claim to have seen the creature in the lake. They have even given it a name—Nessie. Some people say they saw Nessie's huge head. Others say they saw its neck or tail. But no one has ever been able to prove that the creature really exists.

In 1987, scientists wanted to find out if there was truth behind the legend. They used special equipment to search for living things in the lake. They found a lot of salmon and other fish, but no monster.

1 The best title for this passage is
Ⓐ "Lakes of Scotland."
Ⓑ "The Legend of Nessie."
Ⓒ "Monster Stories."
Ⓓ "Scientists Find Loch Ness Monster."

2 You can guess from the passage that
Ⓐ the Loch Ness Monster is red.
Ⓑ Scotland has only one lake.
Ⓒ many people don't believe in the Loch Ness Monster.
Ⓓ there really is a monster in the lake.

Vocabulary

Synonyms

Read the underlined word in each phrase. Mark the word below it that has the same (or close to the same) meaning.

Sample:
glance over
(A) look   (C) return
(B) try   (D) share

1 the calm ocean
(A) cold   (C) rough
(B) deep   (D) peaceful

2 the final game
(A) hardest   (C) first
(B) last   (D) best

3 stumble over it
(A) trip   (C) hear
(B) fight   (D) leap

4 a timid boy
(A) intelligent (C) shy
(B) tired   (D) happy

5 reply quickly
(A) pull   (C) draw
(B) answer   (D) lock

6 twist the top
(A) touch   (C) close
(B) turn   (D) lift

7 trembling like a leaf
(A) falling   (C) growing
(B) shaking   (D) living

Multiple Meanings

Read each set of sentences. Mark the word that makes sense in both sentences.

Sample:
George lost his new _____ at the park.
I want to _____ the sun set tonight.
(A) book   (C) see
(B) watch   (D) pen

1 The kids lined up in alphabetical _____.
"May I take your _____?" he asked.
(A) line   (C) name
(B) coat   (D) order

2 Hillary threw the ball with all her _____.
The Joneses _____ stop by for a visit.
(A) strength   (C) might
(B) did   (D) may

3 _____ cooled the hot room.
The team's _____ applauded every play.
(A) fans   (C) coach
(B) wind   (D) they

4 All people have a _____ to food and shelter.
Do you know the _____ answer?
(A) next   (C) need
(B) right   (D) best

Reading Skills Practice Test 8
Reading Comprehension

Read each passage. Then, fill in the circle that best completes each sentence or answers each question.

Octopuses live in the world's warm oceans. Their bodies are soft and boneless, but they have tough skin called a **mantle** to protect them. Octopuses have six arms and two legs. They use their eight limbs to catch lobsters, shrimps, clams, and crabs.

1 What is the best title for this passage?
Ⓐ "Life Under the Sea"
Ⓑ "What Fish Eat for Dinner"
Ⓒ "The Octopus"
Ⓓ "How to Catch a Lobster"

2 In this passage, the word **mantle** means
Ⓐ tough skin.
Ⓑ limb.
Ⓒ boneless.
Ⓓ arm.

A. There are five steps to writing a story. The first step is called *pre-writing*. That's when you choose a subject and learn all you can about it. The next step is to write a rough draft of your story. It does not have to be perfect. Then you revise your draft. That means you find ways to make it better. Now you are ready for the fourth step, editing. To edit a story, you correct any mistakes. Finally, you publish, or share, your story. You might read the story aloud or give it to a friend to read.

1 What is the best title for this passage?
Ⓐ "My Favorite Subject"
Ⓑ "Read to a Friend"
Ⓒ "How to Write a Story"
Ⓓ "How to Write a Letter"

2 What should you do first?
Ⓐ Write a rough draft.
Ⓑ Choose a subject.
Ⓒ Publish your story.
Ⓓ Look for mistakes.

3 To publish a story, you
Ⓐ share it with others.
Ⓑ collect information.
Ⓒ write a rough draft.
Ⓓ edit it.

4 You can guess from this passage that
Ⓐ rough drafts must be perfect.
Ⓑ all stories have lots of spelling mistakes.
Ⓒ even kids can publish stories.
Ⓓ only grown-ups can publish stories.

B. When Earth travels in its **orbit** around the sun, it takes 365¼ calendar days to make the trip. But it would be strange to see ¼ of a day on your calendar! So, for three years we save up that ¼ day. By the fourth year, it adds up to a whole day! Then we add that extra day to the month of February. When February has 29 days instead of 28, we call that a leap year.

1 This passage is mainly about
Ⓐ why we have leap year.
Ⓑ the seasons of the year.
Ⓒ who invented the calendar.
Ⓓ why February is cold.

2 Earth travels around the sun in
Ⓐ 365 days.　　Ⓒ 365¼ days.
Ⓑ 366 days.　　Ⓓ 366¼ days.

3 In this passage, the word **orbit** means
Ⓐ ship.　　Ⓒ quickly.
Ⓑ path.　　Ⓓ slowly.

4 Which of the following is an *opinion* about February 29?
Ⓐ It comes once every four years.
Ⓑ It's a special day.
Ⓒ It comes during a leap year.
Ⓓ It follows February 28.

C. Digging through old garbage probably doesn't sound fun to you. But that's exactly what a garbologist does. A garbologist goes to landfills, where trash is buried. The garbologist digs up the trash to find out how long different things take to decompose, or break down into soil. He or she also looks to see what kinds of trash people throw away.

Why do garbologists care so much about other people's trash? They know that too much garbage is bad for the planet. They want to find ways to reduce the amount of trash people **create**.

1 What is the main idea of this passage?
Ⓐ It's not fun to dig through garbage.
Ⓑ *Garbologist* is a silly job name.
Ⓒ Garbologists study garbage to find ways to reduce trash.
Ⓓ Trash is taken to landfills.

2 A landfill is a place where people
Ⓐ live.　　Ⓒ recycle trash.
Ⓑ bury trash.　　Ⓓ grow food.

3 In this passage, the word **create** means
Ⓐ make.　　Ⓒ break down.
Ⓑ dig up.　　Ⓓ decompose.

4 Garbologists dig up trash to
Ⓐ look for buried treasure.
Ⓑ find objects they can sell.
Ⓒ see what kind of trash there is and how long it takes to decompose.
Ⓓ spy on people.

D. Anansi the spider thought that if he had a jar full of wisdom, he would be wiser than anyone. So he walked through his village with a jar, asking the wisest people he knew to put some wisdom in it.

When the jar was full, Anansi decided to hide the jar high up in a tree. He tied a belt around his middle and tucked the jar in front. Then he tried to climb the tree, but the jar kept getting in his way.

Just then Anansi's son came along. "Father," he asked, "shouldn't you tuck the jar in the back of the belt?"

Anansi was annoyed. He had a jar full of wisdom, but even a child was wiser than he was. So after he climbed to the top of the tree, he threw the jar down and smashed it. The wisdom scattered all over Earth. And that is how people got wisdom.

1 The author told this story to tell
Ⓐ a few facts about spiders.
Ⓑ how people got wisdom.
Ⓒ why people use jars.
Ⓓ how people can become smarter.

2 Which happened last?
Ⓐ Anansi smashed the jar.
Ⓑ Anansi collected wisdom in a jar.
Ⓒ Anansi tucked the jar behind him.
Ⓓ Anansi climbed the tree.

3 You would probably find this story in
Ⓐ a book about spiders.
Ⓑ a book about the brain.
Ⓒ a book of folktales.
Ⓓ a nature guide.

E. If you think that computers don't belong on a farm, think again! People have found new ways to make work faster and easier on farms. Here are some uses for a computer on a farm:
• Farmers need to know how much their animals eat. If the animals don't get enough to eat, they won't be healthy. Now, a farmer can put a special collar on each animal. The collar hooks up to a computer that will **alert** the farmer if the animal is not eating enough.
• It can take dairy farmers hours to milk their cows. But a Dutch company has invented a robot that does all the work. When a cow is ready to be milked, it stands next to the robot. A gate closes, and the robot does the milking.

1 In this passage, the word **alert** means
Ⓐ warn.   Ⓒ shout.
Ⓑ hide.   Ⓓ ignore.

2 The passage will likely go on to talk about
Ⓐ farm animals in different countries.
Ⓑ more inventions that help farmers.
Ⓒ how to milk a cow by hand.
Ⓓ what cows eat.

3 What is the main idea of this passage?
Ⓐ Milking cows is hard work.
Ⓑ Computers don't belong on a farm.
Ⓒ Inventions make farm work easier.
Ⓓ Farm animals eat a lot.

Vocabulary

Synonyms

Read the underlined word in each phrase. Mark the word below it that has the same (or close to the same) meaning.

Sample:

creep across the floor
- Ⓐ far
- Ⓒ run
- Ⓑ sneak
- Ⓓ stomp

1 burst the bubble
- Ⓐ blow
- Ⓒ soap
- Ⓑ float
- Ⓓ pop

2 a loud giggle
- Ⓐ sob
- Ⓒ noise
- Ⓑ sneeze
- Ⓓ laugh

3 a foolish idea
- Ⓐ large
- Ⓒ silly
- Ⓑ writer
- Ⓓ singer

4 bright student
- Ⓐ shiny
- Ⓒ smart
- Ⓑ tall
- Ⓓ silly

5 fry a hamburger
- Ⓐ eat
- Ⓒ share
- Ⓑ cook
- Ⓓ taste

6 rotating the globe
- Ⓐ turning
- Ⓒ slowing
- Ⓑ falling
- Ⓓ glowing

7 challenging problem
- Ⓐ ugly
- Ⓒ easy
- Ⓑ hard
- Ⓓ new

Antonyms

Read the underlined word in each phrase. Mark the word below it that means the opposite or nearly the opposite.

Sample:

cheerful child
- Ⓐ happy
- Ⓒ sleepy
- Ⓑ pretty
- Ⓓ sad

1 calm lake
- Ⓐ dry
- Ⓒ stormy
- Ⓑ large
- Ⓓ quiet

2 chilly breeze
- Ⓐ warm
- Ⓒ slight
- Ⓑ strong
- Ⓓ icy

3 contest champion
- Ⓐ umpire
- Ⓒ player
- Ⓑ loser
- Ⓓ winner

4 enjoy the movie
- Ⓐ watch
- Ⓒ like
- Ⓑ show
- Ⓓ dislike

5 recall her name
- Ⓐ forget
- Ⓒ say
- Ⓑ remember
- Ⓓ listen

6 shrinking in size
- Ⓐ shopping
- Ⓒ changing
- Ⓑ teasing
- Ⓓ growing

7 wobbly legs
- Ⓐ young
- Ⓒ sturdy
- Ⓑ short
- Ⓓ old

Name _____ Date _____

Reading Skills Practice Test 9
Reading Comprehension

Read each passage. Then, fill in the circle that best completes each sentence or answers each question.

SAMPLE

Did you ever wonder why your mouth waters when you smell supper cooking or spot a fresh-baked batch of cookies? When you smell or see the food, your senses send a signal to your brain that it's time to eat. Then your brain tells your mouth to start making watery saliva. When you finally take a bite of food, this saliva will make the food **moist**. Wet food is easier to chew and swallow.

1 What is the best title for this passage?
(A) "How to Bake Cookies"
(B) "How Your Brain Works"
(C) "Why Your Mouth Waters"
(D) "Tasty Treats Around the World"

2 In this passage, the word **moist** means
(A) wet.
(B) spicy.
(C) cold.
(D) hot.

A. Police dogs have an important role in fighting crime. Each dog works closely with one police officer. Together, the dog and the officer go through four months of difficult training. Once the training is complete, the dog uses its super-powerful nose to help the officer track down criminals, search for stolen property, and sniff out drugs and other illegal substances. A police dog and its human partner always work as a team. In most cases, a dog even lives at home with its human partner! This helps to keep the **bond** between them strong.

1 In this passage, the word **bond** means
(A) battle.   (C) connection.
(B) job.   (D) house.

2 This passage is mainly about
(A) fighting crime.
(B) police dogs.
(C) dogs' sense of smell.
(D) which dogs make the best pets.

3 A police dog does *not*
(A) track down criminals.
(B) live at the police station.
(C) sniff out drugs.
(D) go through training.

4 You can guess from the passage that
(A) dogs have a strong sense of smell.
(B) all police officers have police dogs.
(C) police-dog training is easy.
(D) police officers and their dogs get tired of one another.

B. Spring comes every year—and so do insects! Each year when the weather gets warmer, gardens, meadows, fields, and forests fill with bugs. There are at least one million different species of insects—more than any other kind of animal. Some of them are as big as the palm of your hand, while others are too small to be seen without a microscope.

Despite their differences, all insects share a few important characteristics. For example, they all have six legs and three body parts—a head, a thorax, and an abdomen. They also all have an exoskeleton, or skeleton on the outside of their body instead of on the inside. This exoskeleton looks like a hard shell. Its job is to protect an insect's delicate digestive system and other internal organs.

1 This passage is mainly about
ⓐ using a microscope.
ⓑ characteristics of insects.
ⓒ spring weather.
ⓓ insects in fields and forests.

2 You can guess from the passage that an eight-legged spider is
ⓐ a large insect. ⓒ a forest insect.
ⓑ not an insect.   ⓓ very rare.

3 An insect's exoskeleton
ⓐ protects it from heat.
ⓑ serves as camouflage.
ⓒ helps it walk.
ⓓ protects its internal organs.

C. A family vacation is a lot of fun, but getting to your vacation spot can be boring! There's nothing like sitting in a car for hours at a time to make a person grouchy and groggy. The next time your family takes a long road trip, try playing one of these traditional travel games.

- **License Plate Game:** To play this game, give each player a pencil and pad of paper. Then try to spot license plates from different states. Whoever finds the most states wins.
- **Beep:** Pick a certain **model** of car (for example, pickup trucks or SUVs) at the start of your trip. Each time you spot that type of car, say "beep" and the color of the vehicle you saw. The first person to say "beep" gets one point. The first person to get 10 points wins the game.

1 In this passage, the word **model** means
ⓐ beauty.   ⓒ type.
ⓑ size.   ⓓ truck.

2 To play the License Plate Game, what should you do first?
ⓐ Pick a type of car.
ⓑ Get one point.
ⓒ Find plates from different states.
ⓓ Give out pencils and paper.

3 To win at Beep you must
ⓐ get 1 point.
ⓑ get 10 points.
ⓒ get more states than other players.
ⓓ get all 50 states.

D. Monday

I overslept and missed my bus.
I didn't have time to eat.
I wore plaid pants with polka dots
And my sneakers on the wrong feet.

I **trudged** to school in the rain
And got there just in time
To hear the teacher announce a test
On math chapters one through nine.

When teacher asked if we had questions,
I raised my hand and said,
"I'm not quite ready for today.
May I please go back to bed?"

By Karen Kellaher

1 Another good title for this poem
might be
Ⓐ "Math Test."
Ⓑ "My Bad Day."
Ⓒ "I Missed the Train."
Ⓓ "Saturday Morning."

2 In this poem, the word **trudged** means
Ⓐ few.   Ⓒ dressed.
Ⓑ overslept.   Ⓓ walked.

3 You can guess that the child in
the poem
Ⓐ is not hungry for breakfast.
Ⓑ needs to buy new sneakers.
Ⓒ didn't study for the math test.
Ⓓ looks good in plaid.

E. Today, many doctors are women, but that was not always the case. Until the middle of the 19th century, only men were permitted to become doctors. A determined woman named Elizabeth Blackwell thought that was unfair—and changed the course of history.

Elizabeth Blackwell was born in England in 1821. She moved to the United States with her family when she was a teenager. When she was 23 years old, Blackwell decided to become a doctor. She applied to many medical schools, but was told "no" again and again. Finally, three years later, a small school in New York accepted Blackwell. Professors at the school never believed she would show up for classes. But Blackwell showed up and studied hard. She graduated at the head of her class.

Once she had her medical degree, Blackwell cared for many patients. She even opened a special hospital for women and children. Years later, she moved back to England and helped women there break into the medical field.

1 What did Blackwell do last?
Ⓐ She opened a hospital.
Ⓑ She applied to medical school.
Ⓒ She moved to England.
Ⓓ She moved to the U.S.

2 You might find this passage in
Ⓐ an atlas.
Ⓑ a nature encyclopedia.
Ⓒ a book of biographies.
Ⓓ a book of poems.

Vocabulary
Which Word Is Missing?
In each of the following paragraphs, a word is missing. First, read the paragraph. Then, find the missing word in the list of words beneath the paragraph. Fill in the circle next to the word that is missing.

Sample:

I had hoped to spend the day in the park. Then, I glanced out the window and saw the day was rainy and _____. So much for my big plans!

Ⓐ sunny   Ⓒ foggy

Ⓑ long   Ⓓ bright

1 Everyone knows that manners are important, but sometimes we all need a reminder. Here are some simple things you can do to be

_____.

Ⓐ polite   Ⓒ rude

Ⓑ first   Ⓓ sweet

2 At the dinner table, you should always use a fork, spoon, and knife to eat your food. And keep in mind that chewing with your mouth open is

_____!

Ⓐ difficult   Ⓒ tasty

Ⓑ lovely   Ⓓ impolite

3 If you would like a dish that is at the other end of the table, kindly ask someone else to pass the item to you. And don't forget to say "thank you"

_____.

Ⓐ loudly   Ⓒ first

Ⓑ afterward   Ⓓ slowly

4 Good manners are important at school, too. When the teacher or another student is speaking, let him or her finish before you respond. No one likes to be _____.

Ⓐ boring   Ⓒ sad

Ⓑ answered   Ⓓ interrupted

5 If you accidentally bump into someone in line in the cafeteria, make sure the person is not hurt. Also, remember to say, "_____ me." This will show that you did not mean to be rude.

Ⓐ watch   Ⓒ excuse

Ⓑ embarrass   Ⓓ dear

6 These pointers tell you what to do in a variety of situations. But above all, keep in mind that having good manners means being considerate of others around you. If you remember that, you'll find that others will truly enjoy your _____.

Ⓐ jokes   Ⓒ stories

Ⓑ company   Ⓓ smile

Reading Skills Practice Test 10
Reading Comprehension

Read each passage. Then, fill in the circle that best completes each sentence or answers each question.

SAMPLE

Some vegetables, such as broccoli, contain nutrients that may help to **prevent** diseases. But many kids don't like to eat these vegetables. Now researchers are looking for ways to make veggies fun. They are trying to create doughnuts and other snacks that contain vegetables.

1 What is the best title for this passage?
Ⓐ "My Favorite Vegetables"
Ⓑ "Making Veggies Fun"
Ⓒ "Doughnuts Are Delicious"
Ⓓ "Why Broccoli Tastes Bad"

2 In this passage, the word **prevent** means
Ⓐ eat.
Ⓑ fry.
Ⓒ keep away.
Ⓓ melt.

A. Before money was invented, people **exchanged** one kind of goods for another. For example, long ago, people used shells, beans, or beads to buy food. Later, people began to make coins out of valuable materials like silver and gold.

Today, we use paper money and coins to buy things. Our money is not made of precious materials, but it is valuable all the same. Each bill or coin is worth the amount printed or stamped on it.

1 The best title for this passage is
Ⓐ "How to Make Money."
Ⓑ "The History of Money."
Ⓒ "Rare Coins."
Ⓓ "Working at a Bank."

2 In the passage, the word **exchanged** means
Ⓐ helped.
Ⓑ traded.
Ⓒ lost.
Ⓓ made.

3 Which of these happened first?
Ⓐ Silver coins were invented.
Ⓑ Gold coins were invented.
Ⓒ Paper money was invented.
Ⓓ People used beads to buy food.

4 You can guess from the passage that
Ⓐ beads have been around a long time.
Ⓑ people have always used paper money.
Ⓒ money was invented in the U.S.
Ⓓ shells are more valuable than coins.

B. People have been flying kites for about 3,000 years. During that time, kites have served many purposes. The Chinese were the first kite makers. One story says that Chinese soldiers attached bamboo pipes to their kites. As wind passed through the pipes, it made a whistling sound that scared away enemies! In 1752, Ben Franklin used a kite to study lightning. And in the early 1900s, the Wright brothers used kites to help design the first airplane.

1 What did Chinese soldiers attach to their kites?
Ⓐ lightning rods
Ⓑ bamboo pipes
Ⓒ silver flutes
Ⓓ box kites

2 This passage is mostly about
Ⓐ kites as weapons of war.
Ⓑ the history of bamboo.
Ⓒ the ways kites have been used.
Ⓓ Ben Franklin.

3 Which happened last?
Ⓐ The Wright brothers used kites.
Ⓑ The Chinese began making kites.
Ⓒ Ben Franklin studied lightning.
Ⓓ Chinese soldiers used kites in battle.

4 You can guess from this passage that
Ⓐ Chinese soldiers won many battles.
Ⓑ kites have always been for kids.
Ⓒ kites have had many uses.
Ⓓ Ben Franklin owned many kites.

C. Taking care of your teeth is important. It can help prevent tooth decay and gum disease. Good tooth care includes brushing and flossing every day, visiting your dentist, and eating healthful foods. To brush your teeth, follow these steps:
1. Get a toothbrush with soft bristles.
2. Place a small amount of toothpaste on the brush.
3. Place the toothbrush against your teeth at an angle.
4. To brush the front and back of your teeth, move the brush back and forth or in small circles.
5. Scrub back and forth on the part of your teeth you use to chew.
6. Brush your tongue to remove tiny **particles** of food.
7. Rinse your mouth with water or mouthwash.

1 In this passage, the word **particles** means
Ⓐ colors.   Ⓒ bites.
Ⓑ pieces.   Ⓓ eats.

2 Before brushing, you should
Ⓐ rinse with mouthwash.
Ⓑ wash your face.
Ⓒ drink cold water.
Ⓓ get toothpaste.

3 Poor tooth care can cause
Ⓐ a bad diet.
Ⓑ soft bristles on your toothbrush.
Ⓒ healthy teeth.
Ⓓ gum disease.

D. Frogs have lived on this planet for millions of years. But recently, scientists have noticed that certain types of frogs are disappearing. Some species have even become extinct. What's the problem? Experts have two **theories**:

- Ruined homes: Many frogs live in ponds or other wet areas. People have dried up these areas in order to build roads or buildings. Some other frogs live in forests. Many forests have been destroyed so that people can use the land. That leaves fewer places for frogs to live.
- Pollution: Chemicals get into the ponds and lands where many frogs live. Many scientists believe that the chemicals make frogs sick.

1 In this passage, the word **theories** means
- Ⓐ scientists.
- Ⓒ habitats.
- Ⓑ lily pads.
- Ⓓ ideas.

2 This passage is mostly about
- Ⓐ why frogs are disappearing.
- Ⓑ where frogs live.
- Ⓒ scientists who study frogs.
- Ⓓ pollution.

3 Frogs have fewer places to live because
- Ⓐ scientists have chased them away.
- Ⓑ oceans have dried up.
- Ⓒ people have destroyed their homes.
- Ⓓ too many baby frogs have been born.

E. The Old Lady Who Swallowed a Fly

I know an old lady who swallowed a fly.
I don't know why she swallowed a fly.
Perhaps she'll die.

I know on old lady who swallowed a spider.
It wiggled, and jiggled, and tickled inside her.
She swallowed the spider to catch the fly.
I don't know why she swallowed the fly.
Maybe she'll die.

I know an old lady who swallowed a bird.
How absurd to swallow a bird!
She swallowed the bird to catch the spider
That wiggled, and jiggled, and tickled inside her.
She swallowed the spider to catch the fly.
I don't know why she swallowed the fly.
I guess she'll die.

1 In this song, the word **perhaps** means
- Ⓐ definitely.
- Ⓒ unlikely.
- Ⓑ maybe.
- Ⓓ always.

2 The second item the old lady swallowed was
- Ⓐ a bird.
- Ⓒ a spider.
- Ⓑ a fly.
- Ⓓ a rat.

3 The next verse will probably tell
- Ⓐ why the old lady swallowed the fly.
- Ⓑ where the old lady lived.
- Ⓒ what the lady ate to catch the bird.
- Ⓓ what flies and spiders eat.

Vocabulary
Which Word Is Missing?

In each of the following paragraphs, a word is missing. First, read the paragraph. Then, find the missing word in the list of words beneath the paragraph. Fill in the circle next to the word that is missing.

Sample:

I want to go for a bike ride. But first, I'll put on my _____. It is not safe to ride without one.

(A) book   (C) shoes
(B) raincoat   (D) helmet

1 Cheetahs live on the plains of Africa. Like the lion and the _____, the cheetah is a cat. But don't be fooled: Cheetahs are a lot bigger and faster than your pet kitten at home!

(A) dog   (C) rabbit
(B) leopard   (D) hamster

2 Cheetahs are meat eaters. That means they have to _____ and kill smaller animals to survive. Cheetahs often hunt gazelles.

(A) wash   (C) stalk
(B) ride   (D) defend

3 The gazelle is an animal that looks a little like a deer. Gazelles are very fast runners. Luckily for the cheetah, it is even more _____ than a gazelle. Once a cheetah gets close to a gazelle, it can easily catch the creature and eat it.

(A) hungry   (C) swift
(B) pretty   (D) spotted

4 In fact, the cheetah is the fastest land animal in the world—faster than a grizzly bear or an Olympic athlete. At top speed, a cheetah runs even faster than some people drive their cars. Luckily, drivers don't have to deal with cheetahs racing down the _____.

(A) cabin   (C) lawn
(B) highway   (D) river

5 Another big cat—the lion—is sometimes called the King of Beasts. It lives in Africa, too. Although cheetahs are faster than lions, lions are much bigger and more powerful. What they lack in speed, they make up for in _____. The lion really uses its muscles.

(A) strength   (C) humor
(B) smell   (D) brains

6 A lion's big _____ might mean that it's showing you its teeth. Or, it might be just tired. To stay as strong as they are, lions need a lot of rest. Sometimes, they sleep 21 hours a day!

(A) mane   (C) muscle
(B) yawn   (D) cage

Tested Skills	Item Numbers				
	Practice Test 1	Practice Test 2	Practice Test 3	Practice Test 4	Practice Test 5
Ask and answer questions to demonstrate understanding of a text, referring explicitly to the text as the basis for the answers.	A1, A4, C1, E2	A2, B2, B4	A2, C2, E4	A1, E2	A3, B2, B3, C1, D1, E2
Determine the main idea of a text; recount the key details and explain how they support the main idea.	B1	A1, B3, E1	B1, C1, E1	B1, C1, D1	A2, B1, C2, D2
Describe the relationship between a series of historical events, scientific ideas or concepts, or steps in technical procedures in a text, using language that pertains to time, sequence, and cause/effect.	B2	C2, E2	A3	D3	
Determine the meaning of general academic domain-specific words and phrases in a text relevant to a *grade 3 topic* or *subject area*.	A2, C2, E1	A3, B1, D1	A1, B3, D1, E3	A2, B2, E1	A1, C3, D3
Use text features and search tools to locate information relevant to a given topic efficiently.	E4	C3	E2		
Distinguish their own point of view from that of the author of a text.	C3, D2	E3	C3	A4, E3	E3
Use information gained from illustrations and the words in a text to demonstrate understanding of the text.	A3, B3, E3	C1, D2	A4, B2, B4, D3	A3, B3, C2, D2	A4, E1
Describe the logical connection between particular sentences and paragraphs in a text (e.g., comparison, cause/effect, first/second/third in a sequence).	D1	D3	D2	C3	C4, D4
Know and apply grade-level phonics and word analysis skills in decoding words.	Synonyms 1–7, Antonyms 1–7	Synonyms 1–7, Antonyms 1–7	Synonyms 1–7, Antonyms 1–7	Which Word is Missing? 1–7	Synonyms 1–7, Antonyms 1–7
Decode multisyllable words.			B2		
Use context to confirm or self-correct word recognition and understanding, rereading as necessary.					

Tested Skills	Item Numbers				
	Practice Test 6	Practice Test 7	Practice Test 8	Practice Test 9	Practice Test 10
Ask and answer questions to demonstrate understanding of a text, referring explicitly to the text as the basis for the answers.	A1, A2, A4, B2, C1, D2	A3, C1, C2, D1, E1, E2	A1, A3, B2, C4, D1, D3	A3, A4, B2, D1,	A1, B1
Determine the main idea of a text; recount the key details and explain how they support the main idea.	B1, D1	A1, B1	B1, C1, E3	A1, B1	B2, D2
Describe the relationship between a series of historical events, scientific ideas or concepts, or steps in technical procedures in a text, using language that pertains to time, sequence, and cause/effect.	A4	D4	A2	C3, E1	B2, D2
Determine the meaning of general academic domain-specific words and phrases in a text relevant to a *grade 3 topic* or *subject area*.	A3, D3	A2, D2	B3, C3, E1	A2, C1, D2	A2, C1, D1, E1
Use text features and search tools to locate information relevant to a given topic efficiently.	E3	B2	C2		E2
Distinguish their own point of view from that of the author of a text.	A5, D4	D3	B4		
Use information gained from illustrations and the words in a text to demonstrate understanding of the text.	C3	B3	A4	B3, D3, E2	A4, B4
Describe the logical connection between particular sentences and paragraphs in a text (e.g., comparison, cause/effect, first/second/third in a sequence).	B4, C2, E1, E2	A4	D2, E2	C2	C2, E3
Know and apply grade-level phonics and word analysis skills in decoding words.	Synonyms 1–7, Multiple Meanings 1–4	Synonyms 1–7, Multiple Meanings 1–4	Synonyms 1–7, Antonyms 1–7	Which Word is Missing? 1–6	Which Word is Missing? 1–6
Decode multisyllable words.					
Use context to confirm or self-correct word recognition and understanding, rereading as necessary.	B3				

ANSWER KEY

Practice Test 1
Reading Comprehension
Sample: **1.** C **2.** B
A: 1. D **2.** A **3.** C **4.** A
B: 1. B **2.** A **3.** B
C: 1. C **2.** D **3.** C
D: 1. C **2.** C
E: 1. A **2.** C **3.** B **4.** D

Vocabulary
Synonyms, Sample: B
1. C **2.** B **3.** B **4.** A **5.** D **6.** B **7.** C
Antonyms, Sample: D
1. A **2.** C **3.** B **4.** C **5.** A **6.** D **7.** A

Practice Test 2
Reading Comprehension
Sample: **1.** C **2.** B
A: 1. A **2.** D **3.** B
B: 1. A **2.** B **3.** B **4.** B
C: 1. B **2.** A **3.** D
D: 1. C **2.** A **3.** B
E: 1. D **2.** B **3.** C

Vocabulary
Synonyms, Sample: B
1. A **2.** C **3.** C **4.** D **5.** C **6.** A **7.** C
Antonyms, Sample: D
1. A **2.** D **3.** C **4.** B **5.** C **6.** B **7.** D

Practice Test 3
Reading Comprehension
Sample: **1.** B **2.** C
A: 1. C **2.** B **3.** D **4.** B
B: 1. B **2.** D **3.** A **4.** B
C: 1. C **2.** C **3.** B
D: 1. A **2.** B **3.** C
E: 1. C **2.** A **3.** A **4.** B

Vocabulary
Synonyms, Sample: C
1. D **2.** C **3.** C **4.** A **5.** B **6.** B **7.** C
Antonyms, Sample: D
1. B **2.** C **3.** B **4.** A **5.** C **6.** A **7.** B

Practice Test 4
Reading Comprehension
Sample: **1.** C **2.** A
A: 1. B **2.** D **3.** A **4.** C
B: 1. C **2.** A **3.** B
C: 1. C **2.** C **3.** D
D: 1. D **2.** A **3.** B
E: 1. A **2.** B **3.** D

Vocabulary
Which Word Is Missing?, Sample: C
1. A **2.** D **3.** C **4.** B **5.** C **6.** B **7.** A

Practice Test 5
Reading Comprehension
Sample: **1.** C **2.** A
A: 1. D **2.** B **3.** A **4.** D
B: 1. B **2.** A **3.** D
C: 1. D **2.** C **3.** B **4.** D
D: 1. B **2.** A **3.** B **4.** C
E: 1. C **2.** C **3.** D

Vocabulary
Synonyms, Sample: D
1. B **2.** C **3.** A **4.** D **5.** A **6.** A **7.** D
Multiple Meanings, Sample: A
1. C **2.** D **3.** A **4.** B

Practice Test 6
Reading Comprehension
Sample: **1.** B **2.** C
A: 1. C **2.** B **3.** D **4.** A **5.** B
B: 1. B **2.** C **3.** A **4.** C
C: 1. D **2.** B **3.** A
D: 1. A **2.** D **3.** B **4.** D
E: 1. B **2.** D **3.** C

Vocabulary
Synonyms, Sample: D
1. B **2.** C **3.** D **4.** B **5.** A **6.** A **7.** D
Multiple Meanings, Sample: C
1. B **2.** D **3.** B **4.** C

ANSWER KEY

Practice Test 7
Reading Comprehension
Sample: **1.** B **2.** C
A: 1. D **2.** A **3.** B **4.** B
B: 1. D **2.** C **3.** B
C: 1. B **2.** C
D: 1. B **2.** C **3.** A **4.** C
E: 1. B **2.** C

Vocabulary
Synonyms, Sample: A
1. D **2.** B **3.** A **4.** C **5.** B **6.** B **7.** B
Multiple Meanings, Sample: B
1. D **2.** C **3.** A **4.** B

Practice Test 8
Reading Comprehension
Sample: **1.** C **2.** A
A: 1. C **2.** B **3.** A **4.** C
B: 1. A **2.** C **3.** B **4.** B
C: 1. C **2.** B **3.** A **4.** C
D: 1. B **2.** A **3.** C
E: 1. A **2.** B **3.** C

Vocabulary
Synonyms, Sample: B
1. D **2.** D **3.** C **4.** C **5.** B **6.** A **7.** B
Antonyms, Sample: D
1. C **2.** A **3.** B **4.** D **5.** A **6.** D **7.** C

Practice Test 9
Reading Comprehension
Sample: **1.** C **2.** A
A: 1. C **2.** B **3.** B **4.** A
B: 1. B **2.** B **3.** D
C: 1. C **2.** D **3.** B
D: 1. B **2.** D **3.** C
E: 1. C **2.** C

Vocabulary
Which Word Is Missing?, Sample: C
1. A **2.** D **3.** B **4.** D **5.** C **6.** B

Practice Test 10
Reading Comprehension
Sample: **1.** B **2.** C
A: 1. B **2.** B **3.** D **4.** A
B: 1. B **2.** C **3.** A **4.** C
C: 1. B **2.** D **3.** D
D: 1. D **2.** A **3.** C
E: 1. B **2.** C **3.** C

Vocabulary
Which Word Is Missing?, Sample: D
1. B **2.** C **3.** C **4.** B **5.** A **6.** B